PRACTICAL GUIDE TO KOTLIN

1.Introduction to Kotlin

Kotlin is a modern programming language that has gained popularity in recent years due to its simplicity, expressiveness, and interoperability with Java. Originally developed by JetBrains, the creators of the popular IntelliJ IDEA IDE, Kotlin is now officially supported by Google as a first-class language for Android development.

One of the key features of Kotlin is its conciseness. With Kotlin, you can achieve the same functionality with less code compared to Java, making it easier to read and maintain. The language is also designed to be safer than Java, with features such as null safety and type interference that help prevent common errors. In addition, Kotlin has support for functional programming paradigms, making it more versatile and powerful than Java in some cases.

Another advantage of Kotlin is its seamless interoperability with Java. Since Kotlin is fully compatible with Java, you can use Kotlin and Java code in the same project without any issues. This means that you can gradually migrate your existing Java codebase to Kotlin without having to rewrite everything from scratch. Kotlin also has excellent support for Java libraries, so you can leverage the vast ecosystem of Java libraries in your Kotlin projects.

In terms of tooling, Kotlin has excellent support in popular IDEs such as IntelliJ IDEA, Android Studio, and Eclipse. The language is fully integrated with these IDEs, providing features like code completion, refactoring, and debugging support. This makes Kotlin a great choice for developers who are already using these IDEs for their Java development.

Kotlin is also supported by a strong and active community. There are many online resources available for learning Kotlin, including official documentation, tutorials, and community forums. The Kotlin language is constantly evolving, with regular updates and new features being added to the language. This means that developers can always stay up to date with the latest developments in the Kotlin ecosystem.

In conclusion, Kotlin is a modern and powerful programming language that offers many advantages over Java. With its conciseness, safety, interoperability, and support for functional programming, Kotlin is a great choice for developers looking to improve their productivity and write more reliable code. Whether you are a beginner or an experienced developer, Kotlin is definitely worth exploring for your next project.

2.Installation of Kotlin

Kotlin is a popular programming language that has gained a lot of attention in recent years. It is a statically-typed programming language that runs on the Java Virtual Machine (JVM). Kotlin is known for its conciseness, safety, and interoperability with Java. In this guide, we will walk you through the installation process of Kotlin on various platforms.

Installing Kotlin on Windows:

To install Kotlin on Windows, follow these steps:

1. Download the Kotlin compiler from the official Kotlin website (https://kotlinlang.org/).
2. Once the download is complete, run the installer and follow the on-screen instructions.
3. After the installation is complete, open a command prompt and type "kotlin" to verify that the Kotlin compiler is installed correctly.

Installing Kotlin on macOS:

To install Kotlin on macOS, follow these

steps:

1. Install Homebrew if you have not already done so. Homebrew is a package manager for macOS that makes it easy to install and manage software.
2. Open a terminal and type the following command to install Kotlin using Homebrew:

brew install kotlin

3. After the installation is complete, you can verify that Kotlin is installed by typing "kotlin" in the terminal.

Installing Kotlin on Linux:

To install Kotlin on Linux, follow these steps:

1. Open a terminal and type the following command to install Kotlin using SDKMAN (Software Development Kit Manager):

sdk install kotlin

2. After the installation is complete, you can verify that Kotlin is installed by typing "kotlin" in the terminal.

Integrating Kotlin with an IDE:

Integrating Kotlin with an Integrated Development Environment (IDE) can make the development process much easier. Kotlin is supported by popular IDEs such as IntelliJ IDEA, Android Studio, and Visual Studio Code.

To integrate Kotlin with IntelliJ IDEA, follow these steps:

1. Download and install IntelliJ IDEA from the official website (https://www.jetbrains.com/idea/).
2. Open IntelliJ IDEA and go to File > New > Project.
3. Select Kotlin from the list of available project types and follow the on-screen instructions to create a new Kotlin project.
4. You can start writing Kotlin code in the editor and run your programs directly from IntelliJ IDEA.

To integrate Kotlin with Android Studio, follow these steps:

1. Download and install Android Studio from the official website (https://developer.android.com/studio/).
2. Create a new Android project or open an

existing one.
3. Android Studio has built-in support for Kotlin, so you can start writing Kotlin code in your Android project.

To integrate Kotlin with Visual Studio Code, follow these steps:

1. Download and install Visual Studio Code from the official website (https://code.visualstudio.com/).
2. Install the Kotlin Language extension for Visual Studio Code from the Marketplace.
3. Open a Kotlin file in Visual Studio Code and start writing Kotlin code.

Writing your first Kotlin program:

Now that you have installed Kotlin and set up your IDE, it's time to write your first Kotlin program. Here is a simple "Hello, World!" program in Kotlin:

```kotlin
fun main() {
    println("Hello, World!")
}
```

Save the above code in a Kotlin file with the

extension .kt (e.g., HelloWorld.kt) and run the program to see the output.

Congratulations, you have successfully installed Kotlin and written your first Kotlin program! Kotlin is a versatile language that can be used for a wide range of applications, from mobile development to web development. Explore the features of Kotlin and start building your own projects with this powerful programming language.

3.Basic syntax of Kotlin

Variables and Constants
Variables in Kotlin are declared using the
keyword "var" followed by the variable name
and its type. Constants, on the other hand, are
declared using the keyword "val". Here is an
example of how you can declare a variable
and a constant in Kotlin:

```kotlin
var age: Int = 30
val name: String = "John"
```

In Kotlin, you can also declare variables
without specifying their type, as the compiler
can often infer the type based on the value
assigned to the variable. For example:

```kotlin
var count = 10
```

Data Types
Kotlin supports all the basic data types such as
Int, Long, Float, Double, Boolean, Char, and
String. Additionally, Kotlin also has special

data types such as arrays and lists. Here is an example of how you can declare an array in Kotlin:

```kotlin
val numbers = arrayOf(1, 2, 3, 4, 5)
```

Control Flow
Kotlin supports all the usual control flow statements such as if-else, for loops, while loops, and when expressions. Here is an example of an if-else statement in Kotlin:

```kotlin
val x = 10
if (x > 5) {
    println("x is greater than 5")
} else {
    println("x is less than or equal to 5")
}
```

Functions
Functions in Kotlin are declared using the keyword "fun" followed by the function name and parameters. Here is an example of how you can declare a simple function in Kotlin:

```kotlin
```

```kotlin
fun greet(name: String) {
    println("Hello, $name!")
}
```

You can call the function like this:

```kotlin
greet("Alice")
```

Classes and Objects
Kotlin is an object-oriented language, and you can define classes and create objects just like in Java. Here is an example of how you can define a class in Kotlin:

```kotlin
class Person(val name: String, val age: Int) {
    fun greet() {
        println("Hello, my name is $name and I am $age years old.")
    }
}
```

You can create an object of this class like this:

```kotlin
val person = Person("Alice", 25)
```

```
person.greet()
```

Null Safety
One of the key features of Kotlin is its built-in support for null safety. By default, variables in Kotlin cannot be null unless you explicitly declare them as nullable using the "?" operator. Here is an example of how you can declare a nullable variable in Kotlin:

```kotlin
var nullable: String? = null
```

To safely access the value of a nullable variable, you can use the safe call operator "?." like this:

```kotlin
val length = nullable?.length
```

In this way, you can avoid null pointer exceptions in your code.

Kotlin is a powerful and modern programming language that offers a wide range of features and capabilities. By understanding the basic syntax of Kotlin, you can start writing Kotlin code and leverage its benefits in your projects. I hope this article has provided you with a good overview of Kotlin's basic syntax and how to use it in your programming endeavors.

4.Variables and Data Types in Kotlin

Kotlin is a modern programming language that is widely used for developing Android applications, web applications, and server-side applications. One of the key features that make Kotlin popular among developers is its flexibility when it comes to declaring variables and data types. In this article, we will explore the different types of variables and data types available in Kotlin, and how to use them in your programs.

1. Variables in Kotlin
In Kotlin, variables are used to store data values that can be later accessed and manipulated in a program. Variables are declared using the 'var' and 'val' keywords. The 'var' keyword is used to declare mutable variables, which means that the value of the variable can be changed later in the program. On the other hand, the 'val' keyword is used to declare immutable variables, which means that the value of the variable cannot be changed once it is assigned.

Here is an example of how to declare variables in Kotlin:
```
```

```
var age: Int = 25 // mutable variable
val name: String = "John" // immutable
variable
```


2. Data Types in Kotlin

Kotlin supports a wide range of data types that can be used to store different kinds of values in a program. Some of the basic data types supported by Kotlin are:
- Int: Used to store integer values.
- Long: Used to store long integer values.
- Float: Used to store floating-point values.
- Double: Used to store double-precision floating-point values.
- Boolean: Used to store true or false values.
- Char: Used to store single characters.
- String: Used to store sequences of characters.

Here is an example of how to declare variables of different data types in Kotlin:
```

var age: Int = 25
var height: Double = 5.11
var isStudent: Boolean = true
var letter: Char = 'A'
var name: String = "Alice"
```

3. Type Inference
One of the key features of Kotlin is its ability to infer the data type of a variable based on the value assigned to it. This means that you do not always have to explicitly specify the data type of a variable when declaring it. Kotlin will automatically infer the data type based on the value assigned to the variable.

Here is an example of type inference in Kotlin:

```
var age = 25 // Kotlin infers the data type as Int
var height = 5.11 // Kotlin infers the data type as Double
var isStudent = true // Kotlin infers the data type as Boolean
var letter = 'A' // Kotlin infers the data type as Char
var name = "Alice" // Kotlin infers the data type as String
```

4. Nullable Data Types
In Kotlin, you can also declare variables as nullable, which means that the variable can store a null value in addition to its data type. This is useful when you are not sure if a variable will have a value or not. To declare a

nullable variable, you can use the '?' symbol after the data type.

Here is an example of how to declare a nullable variable in Kotlin:
```

var age: Int? = null
var name: String? = null
```


5. Arrays and Collections
Kotlin also supports arrays and collections, which are used to store multiple values of the same data type or different data types. Arrays are used to store fixed-size collections of elements of the same data type, while collections are used to store dynamic-size collections of elements.

Here is an example of how to declare an array and a list in Kotlin:
```

var numbers = arrayOf(1, 2, 3, 4, 5) // array of integers
var names = listOf("Alice", "Bob", "Charlie") // list of strings
```

6. Enumerations
Enums are a special data type in Kotlin that

allow you to define a set of named constants. Enumerations are useful when you have a fixed set of values that a variable can take on. Enums in Kotlin are declared using the 'enum class' keyword.

Here is an example of how to declare an enumeration in Kotlin:
```
enum class Gender {
    MALE, FEMALE, OTHER
}

var gender = Gender.MALE
```

7. Type Aliases
Type aliases are used to create alternative names for existing data types in Kotlin. This can be useful when you want to make your code more readable and maintainable. Type aliases are declared using the 'typealias' keyword.

Here is an example of how to declare a type alias in Kotlin:
```
typealias EmployeeId = String
var id: EmployeeId = "EMP001"
```

8. Smart Casts

Kotlin also supports smart casts, which allow you to automatically cast a variable to a more specific data type based on certain conditions. This can be useful when working with nullable types or generic types in Kotlin.

Here is an example of how smart casts work in Kotlin:

```
val age: Any = 25
if (age is Int) {
    println("Age is an integer")
    val ageInt = age // automatically cast to Int
}
```

Kotlin provides a wide range of variables and data types that make it easy to work with different kinds of values in a program. Whether you need to store simple integer values or complex data structures, Kotlin has you covered. By understanding the different types of variables and data types in Kotlin, you can write more efficient and maintainable code in your programs.

5. Kotlin Conditional Constructs

Conditional constructs in Kotlin are essential elements of programming that allow developers to execute code based on certain conditions. These constructs enable developers to create dynamic and responsive applications by controlling the flow of execution based on different scenarios. In this article, we will delve into the various conditional constructs available in Kotlin and explore how they can be effectively utilized in programming.

One of the most commonly used conditional constructs in Kotlin is the 'if' statement. The 'if' statement allows developers to execute a block of code based on a given condition. Here's a simple example of an 'if' statement in Kotlin:

```kotlin
fun main() {
    val number = 10
    if (number > 0) {
        println("The number is positive")
    }
}
```

In this example, the 'if' statement checks if the 'number' variable is greater than 0. If the condition is true, the message "The number is positive" is printed to the console. Otherwise, the code block inside the 'if' statement is not executed.

To add more flexibility to conditional statements, developers can utilize the 'else' clause. The 'else' clause is used to specify a block of code that should be executed when the condition in the 'if' statement is false. Here's an example that incorporates the 'else' clause:

```kotlin
fun main() {
    val number = -5
    if (number > 0) {
        println("The number is positive")
    } else {
        println("The number is non-positive")
    }
}
```

In this example, if the 'number' variable is not greater than 0, the message "The number is non-positive" is printed to the console.

In addition to the 'if' and 'else' statements, Kotlin also supports the 'else if' statement. The 'else if' statement allows developers to check multiple conditions within the same 'if-else' block. Here's an example that demonstrates the use of 'else if' in Kotlin:

```kotlin
fun main() {
    val number = 0
    if (number > 0) {
        println("The number is positive")
    } else if (number < 0) {
        println("The number is negative")
    } else {
        println("The number is zero")
    }
}
```

In this example, the code block inside the 'else if' statement is executed when the first condition is false, but the 'number' variable is less than 0. If all conditions in the 'if-else if-else' block are false, the code block inside the 'else' statement is executed.

Apart from the 'if' statement, Kotlin also provides a concise way to handle conditional logic using the 'when' statement. The 'when' statement is similar to a 'switch' statement in other programming languages and allows developers to evaluate multiple conditions in a single block of code. Here's an example of using the 'when' statement in Kotlin:

```kotlin
fun main() {
    val number = 7
    when (number) {
        1 -> println("One")
        2 -> println("Two")
        in 3..5 -> println("Between three and five")
        else -> println("Other number")
    }
}
```

In this example, the 'when' statement evaluates the value of the 'number' variable and executes the corresponding block of code based on the matching condition. The 'in' keyword is used to specify a range of values that the 'number' variable can fall within.

Kotlin also supports the usage of 'return' statements within conditional constructs. Developers can use 'return' statements to exit a function early based on certain conditions. Here's an example that demonstrates the usage of 'return' statements in Kotlin:

```kotlin
fun checkNumber(number: Int): String {
    if (number > 0) {
        return "Positive"
    } else if (number < 0) {
        return "Negative"
    } else {
        return "Zero"
    }
}

fun main() {
    println(checkNumber(10))
}
```

In this example, the 'checkNumber' function takes an integer input and returns a corresponding string based on whether the number is positive, negative, or zero. The 'return' statements in the 'if-else if-else' block help exit the function early once a condition is met.

Another important aspect of conditional constructs in Kotlin is the usage of 'when' as an expression. The 'when' statement can be used as an expression to assign a value based on the evaluated condition. Here's an example that illustrates this concept:

```kotlin
fun checkNumber(number: Int): String {
    val result = when {
        number > 0 -> "Positive"
        number < 0 -> "Negative"
        else -> "Zero"
    }
    return result
}

fun main() {
    println(checkNumber(-5))
}
```

In this example, the 'when' statement is used as an expression to assign a value to the 'result' variable based on the evaluated condition. This provides a concise and effective way to handle conditional logic in Kotlin.

In addition to the traditional conditional constructs, Kotlin also offers the 'if-else' expression, which provides a more concise way to handle conditional logic. Unlike the 'if-else' statement, the 'if-else' expression returns a value based on the condition evaluated. Here's an example that demonstrates the usage of 'if-else' expression in Kotlin:

```kotlin
fun checkNumber(number: Int): String {
    val result = if (number > 0) {
        "Positive"
    } else {
        "Non-positive"
    }
    return result
}

fun main() {
    println(checkNumber(-3))
}
```

In this example, the 'if-else' expression assigns a value to the 'result' variable based on whether the 'number' variable is positive or non-positive. The expression returns a value that can be directly used or manipulated within the program.

Conditional constructs play a crucial role in programming by allowing developers to create dynamic and flexible applications. By leveraging the various conditional constructs available in Kotlin, developers can effectively control the flow of execution and build responsive software solutions. Whether using the 'if' statement, 'when' statement, 'return' statements, or 'if-else' expressions, Kotlin provides a versatile set of tools to handle conditional logic in a concise and efficient manner.

Understanding and mastering conditional constructs in Kotlin is essential for developers looking to write robust and maintainable code. By exploring and experimenting with the different conditional constructs discussed in this article, developers can enhance their programming skills and create efficient and responsive applications. As Kotlin continues to gain popularity in the software development community, proficiency in using conditional constructs will be a valuable asset for developers seeking to excel in their craft.

6.Cycles in Kotlin

Cycles in Kotlin are an essential programming concept that allows developers to execute a block of code repeatedly based on certain conditions. There are three main types of loops in Kotlin: while loops, do-while loops, and for loops. Each type of loop has its own strengths and use cases, making them versatile tools for solving different programming problems.

While loops in Kotlin are used to execute a block of code as long as a given condition is true. The syntax for a while loop in Kotlin is simple:

```kotlin
while(condition){
    // code to execute
}
```

For example, let's say we want to print the numbers from 1 to 5 using a while loop:

```kotlin
var i = 1
while(i <= 5){
```

```
    println(i)
    i++
}
```

In this example, the while loop will execute as long as the variable `i` is less than or equal to 5. The loop will print the value of `i` and then increment it by 1 on each iteration.

Do-while loops in Kotlin are similar to while loops, but the condition is checked after the block of code is executed. This means that the block of code will always execute at least once, regardless of the condition. The syntax for a do-while loop in Kotlin is:

```kotlin
do {
    // code to execute
} while(condition)
```

For example, let's modify the previous example to use a do-while loop instead:

```kotlin
var i = 1
do {
    println(i)
```

    i++
} while (i <= 5)
```

In this case, the value of `i` is printed first, and then the condition is checked. Since `i` is less than or equal to 5, the loop will continue to execute.

For loops in Kotlin are used when you know the number of iterations in advance. The syntax for a for loop in Kotlin is:

```kotlin
for(item in collection){
    // code to execute
}
```

For example, let's use a for loop to print the numbers from 1 to 5:

```kotlin
for(i in 1..5){
    println(i)
}
```

In this example, the for loop iterates over the range 1 to 5 and prints each value in the range.
```

In addition to these basic loops, Kotlin also provides the ability to use break and continue statements to control loop execution. The `break` statement is used to exit the loop prematurely, while the `continue` statement is used to skip the current iteration and continue with the next one.

```kotlin
for(i in 1..10){
   if(i == 5){
      break
   }
   println(i)
}
```

In this example, the loop will print numbers from 1 to 4 and then exit when `i` is equal to 5.

Loops are a powerful tool in programming, allowing developers to iterate over data structures, manipulate values, and control program flow. Understanding the different types of loops in Kotlin and how to use them effectively is essential for writing efficient and readable code.

Loops are an essential part of programming in Kotlin, allowing developers to execute a block of code repeatedly based on certain conditions. While loops, do-while loops, and for loops each have their own strengths and use cases, making them versatile tools for solving different programming problems. By mastering loops and understanding how to use them effectively, developers can write more efficient and readable code in Kotlin.

7.Kotlin Array

Kotlin is a modern programming language that has gained popularity in recent years due to its concise syntax, interoperability with Java, and advanced features. One of the key features of Kotlin is its support for arrays, which are essential data structures in programming. In this article, we will explore how arrays work in Kotlin and how they can be used effectively in your code.

An array in Kotlin is a collection of elements of the same data type that are stored in contiguous memory locations. Arrays can be one-dimensional or multi-dimensional, meaning they can store elements in a single row or in multiple rows and columns. Arrays in Kotlin are zero-indexed, which means that the first element in the array is at index 0.

To create an array in Kotlin, you can use the arrayOf() function. This function takes the elements of the array as arguments and returns an array with those elements. Here is an example of how to create an array of integers in Kotlin:

```kotlin
```

val numbers = arrayOf(1, 2, 3, 4, 5)
```

You can also specify the data type of the array explicitly by using the arrayOf&lt;Int&gt;() syntax. For example:

```kotlin
val numbers: Array<Int> = arrayOf(1, 2, 3, 4, 5)
```

Arrays in Kotlin are mutable, which means that you can modify the elements of the array after it has been created. You can access elements of an array by indexing into the array using square brackets ([]). For example, to access the third element of the numbers array from the previous example, you can do the following:

```kotlin
val thirdNumber = numbers[2]
```

You can also update elements of an array by assigning a new value to the desired index. For example, to update the second element of the numbers array to 10, you can do the following:
```

```kotlin
numbers[1] = 10
```

In addition to creating arrays using the arrayOf() function, you can also use the Array constructor to create arrays in Kotlin. The Array constructor takes the size of the array and a lambda function that initializes the elements of the array. For example, to create an array of 5 integer elements with each element initialized to its index, you can do the following:

```kotlin
val numbers = Array(5) { it }
```

You can also create multi-dimensional arrays in Kotlin using nested arrays. For example, to create a 2D array of integers with 3 rows and 2 columns, you can do the following:

```kotlin
val matrix = Array(3) { Array(2) { 0 } }
```

In this example, the outer Array constructor creates an array with 3 elements, each of which is initialized with a new inner array of 2 elements, each initialized to 0.

Arrays in Kotlin also provide a number of useful functions and properties that make working with arrays easier. For example, you can use the size property to get the size of an array, the get() function to retrieve an element at a specific index, and the set() function to update an element at a specific index.

Arrays in Kotlin also support various operations such as filtering, sorting, and mapping using the built-in functions provided by the Kotlin standard library. For example, you can use the map() function to transform each element of an array, the filter() function to select elements that meet a certain criteria, and the sort() function to sort the elements of an array.

In addition to standard arrays, Kotlin also provides specialized array types such as IntArray, BooleanArray, and CharArray, which are optimized for specific data types and offer better performance for certain operations.

Overall, arrays are an important data structure in programming, and Kotlin provides a flexible and powerful array implementation that makes it easy to work with arrays in your code. Whether you are working with one-dimensional arrays or multi-dimensional arrays, Kotlin's array support makes it easy to work with collections of elements efficiently and effectively.

Kotlin's array support is a powerful feature that allows developers to work with collections of elements easily and efficiently. By leveraging the various array functions and properties provided by Kotlin, developers can write code that is concise, readable, and maintainable. Whether you are a beginner or an experienced developer, arrays in Kotlin provide a versatile and flexible means of managing data in your programs.

8.Kotlin strings

Strings are sequences of characters that represent text. In this article, we will explore various aspects of working with strings in Kotlin.

1. Creating Strings

In Kotlin, strings can be created using double quotes("") or triple quotes(""""""). Double quotes are used to create a single line string, while triple quotes are used for multi-line strings. For example:

```kotlin
val singleLineString = "This is a single line string"
val multiLineString = """
    This is a multi-line
    string in Kotlin
"""
```

2. String Interpolation

String interpolation is a powerful feature in Kotlin that allows for easy embedding of variables and expressions within strings. This can be done using the "$" symbol. For example:

```kotlin
```

```kotlin
val name = "John"
val age = 30
val message = "My name is $name and I am $age years old"
```


3. String Templates

String templates in Kotlin allow for more complex expressions to be embedded within strings. This can be achieved by using curly braces within the "$" symbol. For example:

```kotlin
val num1 = 10
val num2 = 20
val sum = "The sum of $num1 and $num2 is ${num1 + num2}"
```


4. Concatenating Strings

Strings can be concatenated using the "+" operator in Kotlin. However, it is important to note that string concatenation can be inefficient for large strings due to the creation of new string objects. For better performance, it is recommended to use StringBuilder or StringBuffer. For example:

```kotlin
val firstName = "John"
val lastName = "Doe"
val fullName = firstName + " " + lastName
```

```

## 5. Accessing Characters

Individual characters within a string can be accessed using the indexing operator ([ ]). Strings in Kotlin are zero-indexed, meaning the first character is at index 0. For example:

```kotlin
val text = "Kotlin"
val firstChar = text[0] // 'K'
val lastChar = text[text.length - 1] // 'n'
```


6. String Methods

Kotlin provides a variety of methods to work with strings. Some common methods include:
- length: Returns the length of the string.
- toUpperCase(): Converts the string to uppercase.
- toLowerCase(): Converts the string to lowercase.
- trim(): Removes leading and trailing whitespaces.
- substring(): Retrieves a portion of the string.
- split(): Splits the string into an array based on a delimiter.
- replace(): Replaces characters or sequences within the string.

7. Comparing Strings
```

Strings can be compared in Kotlin using the equals() method or the == operator. It is important to note that the == operator compares the values of the strings, while the === operator compares the references. For example:
```kotlin
val str1 = "Hello"
val str2 = "Hello"

println(str1 == str2) // true
println(str1 === str2) // true
```


8. String Constants
In Kotlin, strings can be defined as constants using the 'const' keyword. This ensures that the string value is known at compile time and can optimize performance. For example:
```kotlin
const val appName = "Kotlin App"
```


9. Raw Strings
Kotlin also supports raw strings, which are enclosed in triple quotes(""""""). Raw strings ignore escape characters and are useful for writing regular expressions, HTML, or multiline strings. For example:
```kotlin
```

```kotlin
val rawString = """
    This is a raw string
    It can span multiple lines
    Special characters like \n are ignored
"""
```

10. String Templates with Raw Strings

String templates can also be used with raw strings in Kotlin. This allows for complex expressions and formatting within raw strings. For example:

```kotlin
val name = "John"
val age = 30
val message = """
    |Name: $name
    |Age: $age
""".trimMargin()
```

Strings are a fundamental part of programming in Kotlin. With powerful features like string interpolation, string templates, and raw strings, Kotlin provides a convenient and efficient way to work with strings in your applications. By understanding the various aspects of strings in Kotlin, you can leverage the language's capabilities to create robust and flexible software solutions.

9.Object-Oriented Programming in Kotlin

Object-oriented programming (OOP) is a programming paradigm that revolves around the concept of objects. It is a way of organizing code in a manner that is focused on the creation of reusable and modular components. Kotlin is a modern programming language that is gaining popularity due to its ability to be used for Android development as well as other platforms. In this article, we will explore how Kotlin leverages the principles of object-oriented programming to create powerful and flexible code.

One of the key concepts in OOP is the idea of classes and objects. A class is a blueprint for an object, defining its properties and behaviors. In Kotlin, classes are defined using the `class` keyword. Here is an example of a simple class in Kotlin:

```
class Person {
    var name: String = ""
    var age: Int = 0

    fun speak() {
```

```
        println("Hello, my name is $name and I
am $age years old.")
    }
}
```

In this example, we have defined a `Person` class with two properties - `name` and `age`, as well as a `speak` method that prints out a greeting. We can create instances of this class using the following code:

```
fun main() {
    val person = Person()
    person.name = "John"
    person.age = 30

    person.speak()
}
```

When we run this code, we will see the output: `Hello, my name is John and I am 30 years old.` This demonstrates how objects can be created from classes in Kotlin.

Another important concept in OOP is inheritance, which allows one class to inherit properties and behaviors from another class.

In Kotlin, inheritance is denoted using the `:` symbol. Here is an example of inheritance in Kotlin:

```
open class Animal {
    fun speak() {
        println("Animal is speaking")
    }
}

class Dog : Animal() {
    fun bark() {
        println("Woof! Woof!")
    }
}
```

In this example, we have defined an `Animal` class with a `speak` method, and a `Dog` class that inherits from the `Animal` class. The `Dog` class also has a `bark` method. We can create instances of the `Dog` class and call its methods as follows:

```
fun main() {
    val dog = Dog()
    dog.speak()
    dog.bark()
```

}
```

When we run this code, we will see the output:
```

Animal is speaking
Woof! Woof!
```


This demonstrates how inheritance can be used to create a hierarchy of classes with shared behaviors in Kotlin.

Encapsulation is another important concept in OOP, which involves bundling the data and methods that operate on the data within a single unit, minimizing the exposure of a class's internal workings. In Kotlin, encapsulation can be achieved using access modifiers. Here is an example of encapsulation in Kotlin:

```
class Account {
    private var balance: Double = 0.0

    fun deposit(amount: Double) {
        if (amount > 0) {
            balance += amount
```
```

```
        }
    }

    fun withdraw(amount: Double) {
        if (amount > 0 && amount <= balance) {
            balance -= amount
        }
    }

    fun getBalance(): Double {
        return balance
    }
}
```

In this example, we have defined an `Account` class with a private `balance` property, and public methods `deposit`, `withdraw`, and `getBalance` to interact with the `balance` property. The `balance` property is only accessible within the `Account` class due to the `private` access modifier. We can use this class as follows:

```
fun main() {
    val account = Account()
    account.deposit(100.0)
    account.withdraw(50.0)
```

```
  println("Balance: $
{account.getBalance()}")
}
```

When we run this code, we will see the output: `Balance: 50.0`, demonstrating how encapsulation can be used to protect the internal state of a class in Kotlin.

Polymorphism is another key principle in OOP, which allows objects to be treated as instances of their parent class, enabling flexibility in the design of code. In Kotlin, polymorphism can be achieved using inheritance and method overriding. Here is an example of polymorphism in Kotlin:

```
open class Shape {
    open fun draw() {
        println("Drawing a shape")
    }
}

class Circle : Shape() {
    override fun draw() {
        println("Drawing a circle")
    }
}
```

```kotlin
class Square : Shape() {
    override fun draw() {
        println("Drawing a square")
    }
}
```

In this example, we have defined a `Shape` class with a `draw` method, and subclasses `Circle` and `Square` that override the `draw` method. We can create instances of the subclasses and call the `draw` method as follows:

```kotlin
fun main() {
    val circle = Circle()
    val square = Square()

    circle.draw()
    square.draw()
}
```

When we run this code, we will see the output:
```
Drawing a circle
Drawing a square
```

```

This demonstrates how polymorphism allows objects to exhibit different behaviors based on their type in Kotlin.

Object-oriented programming is a powerful paradigm that allows for the creation of flexible, modular, and reusable code. Kotlin, with its support for classes, objects, inheritance, encapsulation, and polymorphism, provides a strong foundation for implementing OOP principles in your code. By leveraging these concepts, you can write clean, organized, and maintainable code in Kotlin.

In conclusion, Kotlin's support for object-oriented programming makes it an ideal choice for developing applications that require the use of OOP principles. By understanding and utilizing classes, objects, inheritance, encapsulation, and polymorphism in Kotlin, you can create robust and flexible code that is easier to maintain and extend. Whether you are a beginner or an experienced developer, Kotlin's OOP features can help you build sophisticated and efficient software solutions.
```

10.Kotlin's Inheritance

Inheritance is a fundamental concept in object-oriented programming that allows one class to inherit the properties and behaviors of another class. In Kotlin, inheritance is achieved through the use of the 'class' keyword followed by a colon and the name of the superclass that the subclass is inheriting from.

One of the key features of Kotlin's inheritance model is that all classes in Kotlin are final by default, meaning that they cannot be subclassed unless explicitly marked with the 'open' keyword. This is in contrast to languages like Java, where classes are not final by default and must be explicitly marked as final if they are not intended to be subclassed.

When a class is marked as open, it can then be subclassed using the 'class' keyword followed by the name of the subclass and the 'extends' keyword followed by the name of the superclass. Subclasses can then override properties and methods of the superclass by using the 'override' keyword.

For example, consider the following Kotlin code:

```kotlin
open class Animal {
    open fun makeSound() {
        println("A generic animal makes a sound")
    }
}

class Dog : Animal() {
    override fun makeSound() {
        println("A dog barks")
    }
}
```

In this example, we have a superclass called 'Animal' with a method called 'makeSound' that prints out a generic sound. We then have a subclass called 'Dog' that overrides the 'makeSound' method to print out a specific sound for a dog.

Kotlin also supports the concept of abstract classes, which are classes that cannot be instantiated directly and are intended to be subclassed. Abstract classes are marked with the 'abstract' keyword and can contain abstract properties and methods, which must be implemented by subclasses.

```kotlin
abstract class Shape {
    abstract fun calculateArea(): Double
}

class Circle(val radius: Double) : Shape() {
    override fun calculateArea(): Double {
        return Math.PI * radius * radius
    }
}
```

In this example, we have an abstract class called 'Shape' with an abstract method called 'calculateArea'. We then have a subclass called 'Circle' that implements the 'calculateArea' method to calculate the area of a circle.

Kotlin also supports the concept of interfaces, which are similar to abstract classes but cannot contain any method implementations. Interfaces are declared using the 'interface' keyword and can be implemented by classes using the 'implements' keyword.

```kotlin
```

```kotlin
interface Shape {
    fun calculateArea(): Double
}

class Circle(val radius: Double) : Shape {
    override fun calculateArea(): Double {
        return Math.PI * radius * radius
    }
}
```

In this example, we have an interface called 'Shape' with a method called 'calculateArea'. We then have a class called 'Circle' that implements the 'Shape' interface and provides an implementation for the 'calculateArea' method.

Inheritance in Kotlin plays a crucial role in code reusability and polymorphism, allowing developers to create hierarchies of classes that share common properties and behaviors. By carefully designing class hierarchies and using inheritance effectively, developers can write cleaner and more maintainable code in Kotlin.

11.Types of Kotlin classes

Kotlin is known for its interoperability with Java, which makes it a preferred choice for many developers working on Android applications. One of the key features of Kotlin is its support for classes and objects, which are the building blocks of any program.

There are several types of classes in Kotlin, each serving a different purpose and allowing developers to structure their code in a way that is logical and efficient. In this article, we will explore the various types of classes in Kotlin and how they can be used to create robust and scalable applications.

1. Basic Classes:
Basic classes are the most common type of class in Kotlin and are used to define the blueprint for objects. Basic classes can have properties, functions, and constructors, which define the behavior and state of the objects created from them. For example, consider a basic class called Person that has properties like name, age, and gender, along with functions like greet() and introduce(). This class can be used to create objects representing individual persons in a program.

```kotlin
class Person(val name: String, val age: Int, val gender: String) {
    fun greet() {
        println("Hello, my name is $name")
    }

    fun introduce() {
        println("I am $name, $age years old, and identify as $gender")
    }
}

fun main() {
    val person = Person("John", 30, "male")
    person.greet()
    person.introduce()
}
```

2. Data Classes:
Data classes are a special type of class in Kotlin that are used to hold data and automatically generate certain functions like toString(), equals(), and hashCode(). Data classes are particularly useful when working with classes that are primarily used to hold data without much additional logic. For example, consider a data class called Car that

has properties like make, model, and year. This data class can be used to represent cars in a program without the need to write boilerplate code for toString(), equals(), and hashCode().

```kotlin
data class Car(val make: String, val model: String, val year: Int)

fun main() {
    val car1 = Car("Toyota", "Corolla", 2022)
    val car2 = Car("Honda", "Civic", 2021)

    println(car1)
    println(car2)

    println(car1 == car2)
}
```

3. Sealed Classes:
Sealed classes are a unique feature of Kotlin that allows developers to restrict the types of subclasses that can extend a sealed class. Sealed classes are commonly used in scenarios where a class can have a fixed set of subclasses, and the compiler can enforce that only those subclasses are allowed. Sealed classes are useful for modeling restricted

hierarchies where all possible subclasses are known upfront. For example, consider a sealed class called Result that can have two subclasses - Success and Failure. This sealed class can be used to represent the outcome of an operation with only two possible results.

```kotlin
sealed class Result {
    class Success(val message: String) :
Result()
    class Failure(val error: String) : Result()
}

fun processResult(result: Result) {
    when (result) {
        is Result.Success -> println("Success: $
{result.message}")
        is Result.Failure -> println("Failure: $
{result.error}")
    }
}

fun main() {
    val result1 = Result.Success("Operation
successful")
    val result2 = Result.Failure("Operation
failed")

    processResult(result1)
```

```kotlin
    processResult(result2)
}
```

4. Abstract Classes:
Abstract classes are used in Kotlin to define common behavior for a group of classes without implementing all methods. Abstract classes cannot be instantiated on their own and must be subclassed to be used. Abstract classes have abstract methods, which are methods without a body that must be implemented by subclasses. Abstract classes are useful for defining a blueprint for classes that have a common set of methods, but their implementation may vary. For example, consider an abstract class called Shape that has an abstract method called calculateArea(). This abstract class can be used as a base class for different shapes like Circle and Square, each implementing the calculateArea() method differently.

```kotlin
abstract class Shape {
    abstract fun calculateArea(): Double
}

class Circle(val radius: Double) : Shape() {
    override fun calculateArea(): Double {
```

```kotlin
        return Math.PI * radius * radius
    }
}

class Square(val sideLength: Double) :
Shape() {
    override fun calculateArea(): Double {
        return sideLength * sideLength
    }
}

fun main() {
    val circle = Circle(5.0)
    println("Area of circle: $
{circle.calculateArea()}")

    val square = Square(4.0)
    println("Area of square: $
{square.calculateArea()}")
}
```

5. Inner Classes:
Inner classes are classes that are nested within
another class in Kotlin. Inner classes have
access to the members of the outer class,
which allows them to encapsulate related
functionality and improve code organization.
Inner classes are useful when a class is closely
related to another class and should not be used

independently. For example, consider a class called Outer that contains an inner class called Inner. The inner class can access the properties and functions of the outer class, making it easier to work with related functionality in a single unit.

```kotlin
class Outer {
    val value = 10

    inner class Inner {
        fun display() {
            println("Value from outer class: $value")
        }
    }
}

fun main() {
    val outer = Outer()
    val inner = outer.Inner()

    inner.display()
}
```

6. Nested Classes:
Nested classes are similar to inner classes in that they are defined within another class, but

they do not have access to the members of the outer class. Nested classes are essentially standalone classes that are enclosed within another class for organizational purposes. Nested classes are useful when a class is related to another class but does not need to access its members. For example, consider a class called Team that contains a nested class called Player. The Player class can represent individual players in a team without needing access to the properties of the Team class.

```kotlin
class Team {
    class Player(val name: String, val number: Int)
}

fun main() {
    val player1 = Team.Player("John", 7)
    val player2 = Team.Player("Jane", 10)

    println(player1.name)
    println(player2.number)
}
```

Kotlin offers a variety of class types that allow developers to structure their code in a flexible and efficient manner. By understanding the different types of classes available in Kotlin and how they can be used, developers can create well-organized and maintainable code that is easy to read and understand. Whether it's basic classes, data classes, sealed classes, abstract classes, inner classes, or nested classes, Kotlin provides the tools necessary to build robust and scalable applications. By leveraging the power of classes in Kotlin, developers can write clean, concise, and efficient code that meets the demands of modern software development.

12. Control structures (if, when, for, while) in Kotlin

Kotlin is a versatile and user-friendly programming language known for its concise syntax and powerful features. One of the key aspects of Kotlin is its support for a variety of control structures, including if statements, when expressions, for loops, and while loops. These control structures allow developers to implement conditional logic, iterate over collections, and control program flow with ease. In this article, we will explore each of these control structures in detail and discuss how they can be used effectively in Kotlin programming.

If statements are one of the most basic control structures in Kotlin. They allow developers to execute a block of code conditionally based on a specified condition. The syntax of an if statement in Kotlin is as follows:

```
if (condition) {
    // code to be executed if condition is true
}
```

In this syntax, the condition is a Boolean expression that determines whether the block of code will be executed. If the condition evaluates to true, the code inside the block will be executed. If the condition evaluates to false, the code inside the block will be skipped.

For example, consider the following code snippet:

```
val x = 10

if (x > 5) {
    println("x is greater than 5")
}
```

In this example, the if statement checks if the value of x is greater than 5. Since the value of x is 10, the condition evaluates to true, and the message "x is greater than 5" will be printed to the console.

In addition to the basic if statement, Kotlin also supports else and else-if clauses to handle alternative conditions. The syntax for an if-else statement in Kotlin is as follows:

```
if (condition) {
    // code to be executed if condition is true
} else {
    // code to be executed if condition is false
}
```

In this syntax, the else block is executed if the condition in the if statement is false. Developers can also chain multiple else-if clauses to handle additional conditions. The syntax for an if-else-if statement in Kotlin is as follows:

```
if (condition1) {
    // code to be executed if condition1 is true
} else if (condition2) {
    // code to be executed if condition2 is true
} else {
    // code to be executed if all conditions are false
}
```

When expressions are another powerful control structure in Kotlin that allows developers to replace complex if-else chains with a more concise and readable syntax.

When expressions are similar to switch statements in other programming languages and can be used to evaluate multiple conditions in a single statement.

The syntax of a when expression in Kotlin is as follows:

```
when (expression) {
    value1 -> // code to be executed if expression matches value1
    value2 -> // code to be executed if expression matches value2
    else -> // code to be executed if none of the above conditions are met
}
```

In this syntax, the expression is evaluated, and the block of code corresponding to the matching value is executed. Developers can also use the else block to handle cases where none of the specified conditions are met. When expressions are a great way to simplify complex conditional logic and make code more readable.

For example, consider the following code snippet using a when expression:

```
val day = 2

when (day) {
    1 -> println("Monday")
    2 -> println("Tuesday")
    3 -> println("Wednesday")
    else -> println("Invalid day")
}
```

In this example, the value of the day variable is evaluated, and the corresponding message is printed based on the day of the week. If the value of day is not 1, 2, or 3, the message "Invalid day" will be printed.

For loops are a common control structure in Kotlin used to iterate over a collection of elements. Kotlin provides several ways to implement for loops, including iterating over a range of values, iterating over a collection, and iterating over arrays. The syntax of a basic for loop in Kotlin is as follows:

```
for (item in collection) {
    // code to be executed for each item in the
collection
```

```
}
```

In this syntax, the for loop iterates over each item in the collection and executes the specified block of code for each item. Developers can also use ranges to iterate over a sequence of values. The syntax for a range-based for loop in Kotlin is as follows:

```
for (i in 1..10) {
    // code to be executed for each value of i
from 1 to 10
}
```

In this syntax, the for loop iterates over the values in the range from 1 to 10 (inclusive) and executes the block of code for each value of i. Developers can also specify a step value to control the increment between values in the range.

While loops are another type of control structure in Kotlin used to execute a block of code repeatedly while a specified condition is true. The syntax of a while loop in Kotlin is as follows:

```
while (condition) {
    // code to be executed while condition is
true
}
```

In this syntax, the block of code inside the while loop is executed repeatedly as long as the condition evaluates to true. Developers can use while loops to implement logic that requires repeated execution until a certain condition is met.

Here's an example of a while loop in Kotlin that calculates the sum of numbers from 1 to 10:

```
var sum = 0
var i = 1

while (i <= 10) {
    sum += i
    i++
}

println("The sum of numbers from 1 to 10 is $sum")
```

In this example, the while loop calculates the sum of numbers from 1 to 10 by iterating over each value of i and adding it to the sum. The loop continues to execute while the value of i is less than or equal to 10.

Kotlin provides a variety of control structures, including if statements, when expressions, for loops, and while loops, to help developers implement conditional logic, iterate over collections, and control program flow effectively. By understanding how these control structures work and how to use them in Kotlin programming, developers can write clean and efficient code that is easy to read and maintain. Whether you are a beginner or an experienced developer, mastering these control structures is essential for becoming proficient in Kotlin programming.

13.Functions and lambda expressions in Kotlin

Functions and lambda expressions in Kotlin are powerful tools that allow developers to create reusable code blocks and functional programming paradigms. In this comprehensive guide, we will explore the fundamentals of functions and lambda expressions in Kotlin, as well as their practical applications in real-world programming scenarios.

Functions in Kotlin are defined using the "fun" keyword, followed by the function name and optional parameters. Functions can have a return type specified after a colon (:), or be left as Unit if they do not return anything. Here is an example of a simple function in Kotlin:

```kotlin
fun greet(name: String) {
    println("Hello, $name!")
}
```

This function takes a single parameter, "name," of type String, and prints out a greeting message. Functions can also have default parameter values, allowing developers to specify default values for parameters if they are not provided:

```kotlin
fun greet(name: String = "World") {
    println("Hello, $name!")
}
```

In this example, if no parameter is provided when calling the greet function, it will default to "World." This feature is useful for providing flexibility when calling functions with a variable number of arguments.

Another important concept in Kotlin is higher-order functions, which can take functions as parameters or return functions as results. Lambda expressions are a concise way of defining anonymous functions or function literals in Kotlin. Lambda expressions are defined within curly braces ({}) and can be passed as arguments to higher-order functions or stored in variables.

```kotlin
val sum: (Int, Int) -> Int = { x, y -> x + y }
val result = sum(3, 5)
```

```
println("Result: $result") // Output: Result: 8
```

In this example, we define a lambda expression "sum" that takes two integer parameters and returns their sum. The lambda expression is stored in a variable called "sum" with the type "(Int, Int) -> Int," which represents a function that takes two integers as parameters and returns an integer. We then call the "sum" function with arguments 3 and 5, storing the result in a variable and printing it out.

Lambda expressions can also be used with higher-order functions like map, filter, reduce, and forEach in Kotlin's standard library. These functions operate on collections and allow developers to perform common operations on each element in a collection using lambda expressions.

```kotlin
val numbers = listOf(1, 2, 3, 4, 5)

val squaredNumbers = numbers.map { it * it }
println("Squared numbers: $squaredNumbers") // Output: Squared numbers: [1, 4, 9, 16, 25]
```

In this example, we use the "map" function to apply a transformation on each element in the "numbers" list, squaring each number. The lambda expression "it * it" is passed to the map function, which squares each element in the list and returns a new list of squared numbers.

The "filter" function can be used to select elements from a collection based on a given condition. The condition is specified in the lambda expression, and only elements that satisfy the condition will be included in the resulting list.

```kotlin
val evenNumbers = numbers.filter { it % 2 == 0 }
println("Even numbers: $evenNumbers") // Output: Even numbers: [2, 4]
```

In this example, we use the "filter" function to filter out even numbers from the "numbers" list. The lambda expression "it % 2 == 0" checks if the element is divisible by 2 with a remainder of 0, filtering out only the even numbers.

The "reduce" function can be used to combine all elements of a collection into a single value by applying a specified operation iteratively. The operation is defined in the lambda expression, and the result is accumulated by applying the operation to each element in the collection.

```kotlin
val sumOfNumbers = numbers.reduce { acc, num -> acc + num }
println("Sum of numbers: $sumOfNumbers") // Output: Sum of numbers: 15
```

In this example, we use the "reduce" function to calculate the sum of all numbers in the "numbers" list. The lambda expression "acc + num" adds each element to the accumulator (initially set to 0), resulting in the sum of all numbers in the list.

The "forEach" function can be used to perform a specified action on each element in a collection without returning a result. This function is useful for side effects, such as printing out elements or updating external state within a loop.

```kotlin
numbers.forEach { println("Number: $it") }
```

In this example, we use the "forEach" function to print out each element in the "numbers" list. The lambda expression "println("Number: $it")" is executed for each element in the list, printing out the number with a descriptive message.

Lambda expressions and higher-order functions provide a concise and expressive way to work with functions and collections in Kotlin. They enable developers to write clean and readable code by delegating common tasks to higher-order functions and simplifying function definitions with lambda expressions.

In addition to standard library functions like map, filter, reduce, and forEach, Kotlin also supports function composition using function composition operators like compose and andThen. These operators allow developers to chain multiple functions together to create composed functions that execute in a specific order.

```kotlin
```

```kotlin
val addOne: (Int) -> Int = { it + 1 }
val square: (Int) -> Int = { it * it }

val addOneAndSquare = addOne andThen square
val result = addOneAndSquare(3)
println("Result: $result") // Output: Result: 16
```

In this example, we define two functions "addOne" and "square" that add one to a number and square a number, respectively. We then use the "compose" operator to create a new function "addOneAndSquare" that first adds one to the input and then squares it. Finally, we call the composed function with the input 3, resulting in 16.

Function composition allows developers to combine functions in a modular and composable way, creating reusable and maintainable code. By chaining functions together with composition operators, developers can create complex functions from simpler building blocks, making code more readable and concise.

In conclusion, functions and lambda expressions are essential features of Kotlin that enable developers to write expressive and concise code. Functions allow developers to define reusable code blocks with optional parameters and return types, while lambda expressions provide a concise syntax for anonymous functions and function literals.

Higher-order functions and standard library functions like map, filter, reduce, and forEach enable developers to work with collections in a functional programming style, applying transformations and operations on each element in a collection. Function composition operators like compose and andThen allow developers to chain functions together to create composed functions that execute in a specific order.

By leveraging the power of functions and lambda expressions in Kotlin, developers can write clean, readable, and maintainable code that is both efficient and expressive. Whether it's defining custom functions, working with collections, or composing functions together, Kotlin provides a robust set of tools for functional programming paradigms.

14.Coroutines and Asynchronous Programming in Kotlin

Kotlin provides great support for asynchronous programming through the use of coroutines, which are lightweight threads that can be suspended and resumed. This allows developers to write asynchronous code that is easy to read, write, and maintain.

In this article, we will explore the concept of coroutines in Kotlin and how they can be used for asynchronous programming. We will look at the basics of coroutines, how they work, and how they compare to traditional threading models. We will also discuss some common use cases for coroutines in Kotlin and provide examples to demonstrate their usage.

What are Coroutines?
Coroutines are a way to perform asynchronous operations in Kotlin without blocking the main thread. They are lightweight threads that can be suspended and resumed, allowing for more efficient use of system resources. Coroutines are built on top of Kotlin's suspend functions, which are functions that can be paused and resumed at a later time.

Coroutines allow developers to write code that looks synchronous but runs asynchronously. This makes it easier to write and understand asynchronous code, as it eliminates the need for callbacks or complex threading models. Coroutines are also highly customizable, allowing developers to control how they are scheduled and executed.

How do Coroutines Work?
Coroutines in Kotlin are created using the `launch` function from the `kotlinx.coroutines` library. This function takes a lambda expression as a parameter, which defines the code that will be executed asynchronously. Inside the lambda expression, developers can use suspend functions to pause the coroutine and resume it at a later time.

When a suspend function is called inside a coroutine, the coroutine is suspended and the function's execution is paused. The coroutine can be resumed later once the suspend function has completed its work. This allows coroutines to perform long-running tasks without blocking the main thread.

Coroutines can also be used with other coroutine builders, such as `async` and `runBlocking`, to perform more complex asynchronous operations. The `async` builder is used to create a coroutine that returns a result, while `runBlocking` is used to run a coroutine synchronously.

Comparison to Traditional Threading Models Coroutines offer several advantages over traditional threading models, such as Java's `Thread` and `Executor` classes. One of the main benefits of coroutines is that they are lightweight, which means they consume fewer system resources compared to traditional threads. This makes coroutines more efficient for performing tasks that involve waiting for long periods of time, such as network requests or file I/O operations.

Coroutines are also easier to understand and maintain compared to traditional threading models. With coroutines, developers can write asynchronous code that looks synchronous, making it easier to reason about the flow of the program. Coroutines also eliminate the need for callbacks, which can lead to cleaner and more readable code.

Another advantage of coroutines is that they can be canceled or timed out using the `cancel` and `withTimeout` functions. This allows developers to easily cancel long-running tasks or set a timeout for asynchronous operations, improving the responsiveness of the application.

Common Use Cases for Coroutines
Coroutines can be used in a wide range of applications to perform asynchronous operations. Some common use cases for coroutines in Kotlin include:

1. Performing network requests: Coroutines can be used to make HTTP requests to a server and process the response asynchronously. This allows developers to fetch data from a remote server without blocking the main thread.

2. Handling user input: Coroutines can be used to process user input events, such as button clicks or text input, in a responsive and non-blocking manner. This ensures that the application remains interactive and smooth.

3. Performing database operations: Coroutines can be used to perform database queries and updates in the background, avoiding blocking the main thread and improving the performance of the application.

4. Processing large datasets: Coroutines can be used to process large datasets or perform computationally intensive tasks asynchronously, ensuring that the application remains responsive and performs well.

Example: Using Coroutines for Network Requests
To demonstrate how coroutines can be used for asynchronous programming in Kotlin, let's create a simple example that makes a network request using the `kotlinx.coroutines` library. In this example, we will fetch data from a remote server and display it in a `TextView`.

```kotlin
import kotlinx.coroutines.*
import java.net.URL

fun main() {
    runBlocking {
        val data = fetchData()
        println("Data: $data")
    }
}


suspend fun fetchData(): String =
withContext(Dispatchers.IO) {
    val url =
URL("https://jsonplaceholder.typicode.com/p
```

```kotlin
osts/1")
    val connection = url.openConnection()
    val response =
connection.getInputStream().bufferedReader()
.readText()
    response
}
```

In this example, we have created a coroutine using `runBlocking` and called the `fetchData` function to make a network request. The `fetchData` function is a suspend function that performs the network request in the background using the `Dispatchers.IO` dispatcher. Once the request is completed, the response is returned as a `String`.

Conclusion

Coroutines are a powerful feature of Kotlin that provide a more efficient and easier way to perform asynchronous programming. By leveraging coroutines, developers can write asynchronous code that is easy to read, write, and maintain, without the complexity of traditional threading models.

We have also discussed some common use cases for coroutines in Kotlin and provided an example to demonstrate their usage.

Overall, coroutines are a valuable tool for writing responsive and scalable applications in Kotlin, and developers are encouraged to explore them further in their projects. By using coroutines, developers can take advantage of asynchronous programming in Kotlin to build high-performance and reliable applications.

15.Kotlin Data Structures

1. Arrays: Arrays are a fundamental data structure in Kotlin that can store a fixed-size collection of elements of the same type. To declare an array in Kotlin, you can use the arrayOf() function followed by the elements enclosed in parentheses. For example:

```
```

```
val numbers = arrayOf(1, 2, 3, 4, 5)
```
```

You can access elements in an array by using the index operator []. Arrays in Kotlin are zero-indexed, which means that the first element is located at index 0. You can also iterate over an array using a for loop or other loop constructs.

2. Lists: Lists are another common data structure in Kotlin that represent an ordered collection of elements. Kotlin provides two implementations of lists: MutableList, which allows you to modify the elements, and List, which is read-only. To create a list in Kotlin, you can use the listOf() function followed by the elements enclosed in parentheses. For example:
```

```
val names = listOf("Alice", "Bob", "Charlie")
```

You can access elements in a list by using the get() function with the index as the argument. Lists in Kotlin also support various operations such as adding, removing, and updating elements.

3. Maps: Maps are key-value pairs that allow you to store and retrieve data based on a unique key. In Kotlin, you can create a map using the mapOf() function followed by the key-value pairs enclosed in parentheses. For example:

```
val ages = mapOf("Alice" to 25, "Bob" to 30, "Charlie" to 35)
```

You can access values in a map by using the get() function with the key as the argument. Maps in Kotlin also support operations such as adding, removing, and updating key-value pairs.

4. Sets: Sets are collections that store unique

elements without duplicates. In Kotlin, you can create a set using the setOf() function followed by the elements enclosed in parentheses. For example:

```
val uniqueNumbers = setOf(1, 2, 3, 4, 5)
```

You can perform set operations such as union, intersection, and difference using the standard set operations provided by Kotlin. Sets are useful for eliminating duplicates and ensuring unique values in a collection.

5. Queues: Queues are data structures that follow the First-In-First-Out (FIFO) principle, where elements are added to the back and removed from the front. In Kotlin, you can create a queue using the ArrayDeque class, which provides efficient operations for adding and removing elements at both ends of the queue. For example:

```
val queue = ArrayDeque<Int>()
queue.add(1)
queue.add(2)
queue.add(3)
println(queue.removeFirst())
```

```
```

The ArrayDeque class in Kotlin also provides other useful methods such as peek(), poll(), and offer() for working with queues.

6. Stacks: Stacks are data structures that follow the Last-In-First-Out (LIFO) principle, where elements are added and removed from the top of the stack. In Kotlin, you can create a stack using the Stack class, which provides methods for pushing and popping elements. For example:

```
val stack = Stack<Int>()
stack.push(1)
stack.push(2)
stack.push(3)
println(stack.pop())
```

The Stack class in Kotlin also provides other methods such as peek(), search(), and empty() for working with stacks.

In addition to these basic data structures, Kotlin also provides support for more advanced data structures such as trees, graphs, and heaps through third-party libraries and frameworks. By leveraging these data structures, you can efficiently organize and manipulate data in your Kotlin applications, leading to more scalable and maintainable code.

Kotlin offers a wide range of data structures that can be used to represent and manipulate data in various ways. Understanding these data structures and their implementations is essential for building efficient and reliable Kotlin applications. By mastering data structures in Kotlin, you can optimize your code for better performance and scalability.

16. Kotlin Stream API

One of the key features that Kotlin offers is the Stream API, which allows developers to process collections of data in a flexible and efficient way.

The Stream API in Kotlin is inspired by Java's Stream API, but with a more Kotlin-friendly syntax. It provides a set of functions that allow developers to perform common operations on collections, such as filtering, mapping, aggregating, and more. This makes it easier to write expressive and readable code, while also taking advantage of Kotlin's type safety and null safety features.

One of the most powerful aspects of the Stream API is its ability to work with both synchronous and asynchronous data sources. This means that developers can use streams to process collections stored in memory, as well as data from external sources such as databases or web services. This flexibility allows developers to build scalable and efficient applications that can handle large amounts of data without sacrificing performance.

To demonstrate the power of the Stream API in Kotlin, let's take a look at a simple example. Suppose we have a list of numbers and we want to filter out the even numbers and then calculate the sum of the remaining numbers. Using the Stream API, we can achieve this with just a few lines of code:

```kotlin
val numbers = listOf(1, 2, 3, 4, 5, 6, 7, 8, 9, 10)
val sum = numbers.filter { it % 2 != 0 }
            .sum()

println(sum) // Output: 25
```

In this example, we first create a list of numbers and then use the `filter` function to remove the even numbers from the list. We then use the `sum` function to calculate the sum of the remaining odd numbers. This simple and concise code demonstrates the power of the Stream API in Kotlin to perform complex operations on collections with ease.

Another useful feature of the Stream API is the ability to chain multiple operations together. This allows developers to create complex data processing pipelines that can perform multiple transformations on a collection in a single pass. For example, we can chain together filtering, mapping, and reducing operations to perform a series of calculations on a list of numbers:

```kotlin
val numbers = listOf(1, 2, 3, 4, 5)
val result = numbers.filter { it % 2 != 0 }
            .map { it * 2 }
            .reduce { acc, i -> acc + i }

println(result) // Output: 18
```

In this example, we first filter out the even numbers from the list, then multiply each odd number by 2, and finally calculate the sum of the resulting numbers. This demonstrates how easy it is to build complex data processing pipelines using the Stream API in Kotlin.

In addition to filtering, mapping, and reducing, the Stream API in Kotlin provides a wide variety of other functions that developers can leverage to process collections in different ways. Some of these include functions for sorting, grouping, partitioning, and collecting data. These functions make it easy to perform common data processing tasks with minimal boilerplate code, resulting in more maintainable and readable code.

Overall, the Stream API in Kotlin is a powerful tool that allows developers to process collections of data in a flexible and efficient way. By providing a set of functions for common operations on collections, as well as support for synchronous and asynchronous data sources, the Stream API enables developers to build scalable and performant applications with ease. Whether you are working with small in-memory collections or large external datasets, the Stream API in Kotlin is a valuable tool that can help you streamline your data processing workflow and write cleaner, more expressive code.

17.The DateTime API in Kotlin

The DateTime API in Kotlin is a powerful
tool for working with dates and times in your
applications. This API provides you with a
wide range of functionalities to manipulate
date and time values, format them, and
perform various calculations and operations
on them. In this article, we will explore the
DateTime API in Kotlin in detail and see how
you can use it in your projects.

Creating DateTime Objects:
One of the core functionalities of the
DateTime API in Kotlin is the ability to create
DateTime objects to represent specific dates
and times. You can create a new DateTime
object by providing the date and time
components such as year, month, day, hour,
minute, second, and millisecond. Here's an
example of creating a DateTime object for the
current date and time:

```kotlin
val now = LocalDateTime.now()
```

In this code snippet, we are using the
`LocalDateTime.now()` function to create a

new DateTime object that represents the current date and time. You can also create a DateTime object for a specific date and time by specifying the date and time components explicitly:

```kotlin
val dateTime = LocalDateTime.of(2022, Month.FEBRUARY, 25, 14, 30)
```

In this example, we are creating a DateTime object that represents the date and time of February 25th, 2022, at 2:30 PM.

Manipulating DateTime Objects:
Once you have created a DateTime object, you can easily manipulate it using various methods provided by the DateTime API. For example, you can add or subtract time units such as days, hours, minutes, and seconds to a DateTime object:

```kotlin
val tomorrow = now.plusDays(1)
val nextHour = now.plusHours(1)
```

In these code snippets, we are adding one day to the current DateTime object `now` to get the date and time for tomorrow, and we are adding one hour to the current DateTime object to get the time for the next hour.

Formatting DateTime Objects:
The DateTime API in Kotlin also provides convenient methods for formatting DateTime objects into strings in different date and time formats. You can easily format a DateTime object into a string using a predefined format pattern or a custom format pattern. Here's an example of formatting a DateTime object into a string:

```kotlin
val formatter =
DateTimeFormatter.ofPattern("dd-MM-yyyy HH:mm:ss")
val formattedDateTime =
now.format(formatter)
println("Formatted DateTime: $formattedDateTime")
```

In this code snippet, we are creating a DateTimeFormatter object with a custom format pattern "dd-MM-yyyy HH:mm:ss" to format the DateTime object `now` into a string with the specified date and time format.

Comparing DateTime Objects:
You can also compare DateTime objects to determine their relative order and relationship. The DateTime API in Kotlin provides methods to compare two DateTime objects based on their date and time values. Here's an example of comparing two DateTime objects:

```kotlin
val dateTime1 = LocalDateTime.of(2022, Month.FEBRUARY, 25, 14, 30)
val dateTime2 = LocalDateTime.of(2022, Month.FEBRUARY, 25, 15, 30)

val comparison = dateTime1.compareTo(dateTime2)
if (comparison < 0) {
    println("dateTime1 is before dateTime2")
} else if (comparison > 0) {
    println("dateTime1 is after dateTime2")
} else {
    println("dateTime1 and dateTime2 are equal")
}
```

In this code snippet, we are comparing two DateTime objects `dateTime1` and `dateTime2` based on their date and time values using the `compareTo` method.

Depending on the result of the comparison, we print a message indicating the relative order of the DateTime objects.

Calculating Duration and Period:
The DateTime API in Kotlin also provides functionalities to calculate the duration between two DateTime objects in terms of hours, minutes, seconds, and milliseconds, as well as the period between two dates in terms of years, months, and days. Here's an example of calculating the duration and period between two DateTime objects:

```kotlin
val dateTimeStart = LocalDateTime.of(2022, Month.FEBRUARY, 25, 10, 30)
val dateTimeEnd = LocalDateTime.of(2022, Month.FEBRUARY, 25, 14, 45)

val duration = Duration.between(dateTimeStart, dateTimeEnd)
val period = Period.between(dateTimeStart.toLocalDate(), dateTimeEnd.toLocalDate())

println("Duration: $duration")
println("Period: $period")
```

In this code snippet, we are calculating the duration between two DateTime objects `dateTimeStart` and `dateTimeEnd` using the `Duration.between` method, and we are calculating the period between the two dates using the `Period.between` method.

Working with Time Zones:
The DateTime API in Kotlin also provides functionalities to work with time zones and convert DateTime objects between different time zones. You can specify a time zone when creating a DateTime object or convert a DateTime object to a different time zone. Here's an example of working with time zones in the DateTime API:

```kotlin
val dateTimeUtc =
ZonedDateTime.now(ZoneId.of("UTC"))
val dateTimePst =
dateTimeUtc.withZoneSameInstant(ZoneId.of
("America/Los_Angeles"))

println("UTC Date and Time: $
{dateTimeUtc.format(DateTimeFormatter.IS
O_ZONED_DATE_TIME)}")
println("PST Date and Time: $
{dateTimePst.format(DateTimeFormatter.ISO
```

_ZONED_DATE_TIME)}")
```

In this code snippet, we are creating a DateTime object in the UTC time zone using the `ZonedDateTime.now` method and then converting it to the PST time zone using the `withZoneSameInstant` method.

Handling Leap Years and Leap Seconds:
The DateTime API in Kotlin also takes care of handling leap years and leap seconds, ensuring that your date and time calculations are accurate and reliable. When working with DateTime objects, the API automatically accounts for leap years in calculations involving years and leap seconds in calculations involving seconds.

Summary:
The DateTime API in Kotlin provides a comprehensive set of functionalities for working with dates and times in your applications. From creating and manipulating DateTime objects to formatting, comparing, calculating duration and period, working with time zones, and handling leap years and leap seconds, the DateTime API offers a wide range of features to make working with dates and times easy and efficient.
```

Whether you need to perform simple date and time operations or complex calculations involving multiple time zones, the DateTime API in Kotlin has you covered. With its intuitive and robust functionality, you can handle all your date and time requirements effectively and accurately. So next time you need to work with dates and times in your Kotlin application, remember to leverage the power of the DateTime API to simplify your date and time handling tasks.

18.Kotlin files

A Kotlin file is a source code file written in the Kotlin programming language. Kotlin is a statically typed programming language that runs on the Java Virtual Machine (JVM) and can also be compiled to JavaScript or native code. Kotlin was developed by JetBrains and officially released in 2016 as an open-source language.

Kotlin is designed to be fully interoperable with Java, meaning that existing Java code can be used seamlessly in Kotlin projects and vice versa. This makes Kotlin a popular choice for Android app development, as it allows developers to take advantage of the modern features and syntax of Kotlin while still being able to access the vast ecosystem of Java libraries and frameworks.

In a Kotlin file, you can write classes, functions, variables, and other code elements that make up your program. Kotlin has a concise and expressive syntax that allows you to write clean and readable code. Let's take a closer look at some key features of Kotlin files.

1. Package Declaration:
At the top of a Kotlin file, you can declare the package that the file belongs to. This is done using the "package" keyword followed by the package name. For example:
```

package com.example.app
```


2. Import Statements:
You can import external classes, functions, and other elements into your Kotlin file using import statements. This allows you to use code from other packages without having to fully qualify each reference. For example:
```

import java.util.*
```


3. Class Declaration:
In Kotlin, classes are declared using the "class" keyword followed by the class name. Classes can have properties, functions, and constructors. Here is an example of a simple class declaration in Kotlin:
```

class Person(val name: String, val age: Int)
```


4. Function Declaration:

Functions in Kotlin are declared using the "fun" keyword followed by the function name. Functions can have parameters and return types. Here is an example of a simple function declaration in Kotlin:
```
fun greet(name: String) {
   println("Hello, $name!")
}
```


5. Main Function:
Every Kotlin file can have a main function, which is the entry point of the program. The main function is where the execution of the program starts. Here is an example of a main function in a Kotlin file:
```
fun main() {
   greet("Alice")
}
```


6. Comments:
Comments in Kotlin are used to document the code and provide explanations for other developers. Kotlin supports both single-line and multi-line comments. Here is an example of a single-line comment in Kotlin:
```
```

```
// This is a single-line comment
```

And here is an example of a multi-line comment in Kotlin:
```
/*
   This is a
   multi-line comment
*/
```

7. Extension Functions:
One of the powerful features of Kotlin is extension functions. These allow you to add new functions to existing classes without modifying their source code. Extension functions can be particularly useful for adding utility methods to classes from external libraries. Here is an example of an extension function in Kotlin:
```
fun Int.isEven(): Boolean {
    return this % 2 == 0
}
```

8. Data Classes:
Kotlin provides data classes, which are a convenient way to declare classes that only

hold data. Data classes automatically generate getter and setter methods, as well as implementations of "toString", "equals", and "hashCode" methods. Here is an example of a data class in Kotlin:
```
data class Point(val x: Int, val y: Int)
```

9. Null Safety:
Kotlin is designed to be null-safe, meaning that it aims to prevent null pointer exceptions at runtime. In Kotlin, you need to explicitly declare when a variable can be null by using the nullable type. Kotlin provides a number of safe operators and functions to handle nullable values. Here is an example of how to declare a nullable variable in Kotlin:
```
var name: String? = null
```

And here is an example of using the safe call operator to safely access a property of a potentially nullable variable:
```
val length = name?.length
```

10. Smart Casts:

Kotlin introduces smart casts, which allow you to use an instance of a variable in a different context after it has been checked for a certain type. This can help reduce boilerplate code when working with type checks and casts. Here is an example of using smart casts in Kotlin:

```
val obj: Any = "Hello"
if (obj is String) {
    println(obj.length)
}
```

11. Interoperability with Java:
As mentioned earlier, Kotlin is designed to be fully interoperable with Java. This means that you can use Java code in Kotlin files and vice versa. Many Java libraries and frameworks can be used seamlessly in Kotlin projects, making it easier to migrate existing Java applications to Kotlin.

12. Coroutines:
Kotlin introduces coroutines, which provide a powerful and lightweight way to perform asynchronous programming. Coroutines can be used to perform non-blocking operations, such as network requests or file I/O, without having to manage threads manually.

Coroutines make it easier to write asynchronous code that is both efficient and readable.

13. Testing Frameworks:
Kotlin has a number of testing frameworks available for unit testing, integration testing, and other types of testing. Some popular testing frameworks for Kotlin include JUnit, MockK, and Spek. These frameworks provide powerful features for writing and running tests, making it easier to ensure the quality and reliability of your Kotlin code.

Kotlin files provide a flexible and powerful way to write clean and concise code for a wide range of applications. Whether you are developing Android apps, web applications, or backend services, Kotlin offers a modern and efficient way to create software that is reliable, maintainable, and scalable. By leveraging the rich features of Kotlin, you can take your programming skills to the next level and build high-quality software that meets the needs of your users.

19.Handling Exceptions in Kotlin

Exception handling is a crucial aspect of software development, as it allows developers to gracefully manage unexpected errors and prevent their applications from crashing. In Kotlin, a modern programming language that runs on the Java Virtual Machine (JVM), exception handling is implemented using try-catch blocks, similar to Java.

Kotlin provides a hierarchy of exception classes that represent different types of errors. At the top of the hierarchy is the Throwable class, which is the superclass of all exceptions and errors in Kotlin. Exceptions are further divided into two categories: checked exceptions, which must be caught or declared in the calling method, and unchecked exceptions, which do not need to be caught or declared.

To handle exceptions in Kotlin, developers use the try-catch-finally block. The try block contains the code that may throw an exception, while the catch block is used to catch and handle the exception if it occurs. The finally block is optional and is used to execute code that should always run, regardless of whether an exception is thrown or not.

Here is an example of exception handling in Kotlin:

```kotlin
fun main() {
    try {
        val result = divide(10, 0)
        println(result)
    } catch (e: ArithmeticException) {
        println("Divide by zero error: ${e.message}")
    } finally {
        println("Finally block executed")
    }
}

fun divide(a: Int, b: Int): Int {
    return a / b
}
```

In this example, the divide function attempts to divide two numbers and may throw an ArithmeticException if the second number is zero. The exception is caught in the catch block, where a custom message is printed. The finally block is executed regardless of whether an exception is thrown.

Kotlin also provides the throw keyword, which allows developers to throw custom exceptions. This can be useful for signaling specific errors in their applications. Here is an example:

```kotlin
fun checkAge(age: Int) {
    if (age < 0) {
        throw IllegalArgumentException("Age must be a positive number")
    } else {
        println("Age is valid: $age")
    }
}

fun main() {
    try {
        checkAge(-10)
    } catch (e: IllegalArgumentException) {
        println("Invalid age: ${e.message}")
    }
}
```

In this example, the checkAge function throws an IllegalArgumentException if the age is less than zero. The exception is caught in the catch block, where a custom message is printed.

Kotlin also supports the use of multiple catch blocks to handle different types of exceptions. This allows developers to write specific error-handling code for different types of errors. Here is an example:

```kotlin
fun main() {
    try {
        val data = fetchData()
        println(data)
    } catch (e: IOException) {
        println("IOException: ${e.message}")
    } catch (e: NullPointerException) {
        println("NullPointerException: ${e.message}")
    }
}

fun fetchData(): String {
    // Simulate fetching data from a remote server
    throw IOException("Failed to fetch data")
}
```

In this example, the fetchData function throws an IOException if there is an error fetching data. The exception is caught in the first catch block. If a NullPointerException occurs instead, it will be caught in the second catch block.

In addition to try-catch blocks, Kotlin also provides the use of the try expression, which is a functional way of handling exceptions. The try expression returns a value that can be used in the code, similar to the return statement. Here is an example:

```kotlin
fun divide(a: Int, b: Int): Int {
    return try {
        a / b
    } catch (e: ArithmeticException) {
        0
    }
}

fun main() {
    val result = divide(10, 0)
    println(result) // Output: 0
}
```

In this example, the divide function uses the try expression to handle the ArithmeticException. If an exception occurs, the function returns a default value of 0.

Overall, exception handling is an essential

part of writing robust and reliable code in Kotlin. By using try-catch blocks, throw statements, and try expressions, developers can effectively manage errors and prevent their applications from crashing. It is important to handle exceptions appropriately and provide meaningful error messages to users to improve the overall user experience and maintain the quality of the software.

20.Collections and Maps in Kotlin

Kotlin offre una vasta gamma di funzioni e strutture dati per aiutare gli sviluppatori a scrivere codice efficiente e manutenibile. Tra queste, le collezioni e le mappe rappresentano due potenti strumenti che consentono di gestire e manipolare i dati in modo efficiente.

Le collezioni in Kotlin sono strutture dati che consentono di memorizzare e manipolare un insieme di elementi dello stesso tipo. Esistono diversi tipi di collezioni in Kotlin, tra cui le liste, gli insiemi e le mappe.

Le liste sono collezioni ordinate di elementi che consentono di accedere ai singoli elementi tramite un indice. Le liste possono contenere elementi duplicati e consentono di aggiungere, rimuovere e modificare gli elementi in modo efficiente.

Gli insiemi, invece, sono collezioni non ordinate di elementi unici. Gli insiemi non consentono duplicati e sono utili per gestire un insieme di elementi univoci senza la necessità di mantenerli in un ordine specifico.

Le mappe sono collezioni di coppie chiave-valore che consentono di associare un valore a una specifica chiave. Le mappe sono utili per memorizzare e cercare rapidamente un valore associato a una chiave specifica e offrono operazioni efficienti per l'aggiunta, la rimozione e la ricerca di elementi.

Per creare e utilizzare collezioni in Kotlin, è possibile utilizzare le strutture dati predefinite offerte dalla libreria standard, come ad esempio le liste, gli insiemi e le mappe mutable e immutabili.

Ad esempio, per creare una lista in Kotlin, è possibile utilizzare la funzione listOf() che restituisce una lista immutabile di elementi specificati:

```kotlin
val lista = listOf("elemento1", "elemento2", "elemento3")
```

Per creare un insieme in Kotlin, è possibile utilizzare la funzione setOf() che restituisce un insieme immutabile di elementi unici:

```kotlin
val insieme = setOf("elemento1", "elemento2", "elemento3")
```

```

Per creare una mappa in Kotlin, è possibile
utilizzare la funzione mapOf() che restituisce
una mappa immutabile di coppie chiave-
valore:

```kotlin
val mappa = mapOf("chiave1" to "valore1",
"chiave2" to "valore2")
```

Le mappe di Kotlin consentono di aggiungere,
rimuovere, modificare e accedere agli
elementi utilizzando le funzioni appropriate
offerte dalla libreria standard.

Ad esempio, per aggiungere un elemento a
una mappa, è possibile utilizzare il metodo
put() che associa una chiave a un valore:

```kotlin
mappa.put("chiave3", "valore3")
```

Per rimuovere un elemento da una mappa, è
possibile utilizzare il metodo remove()
specificando la chiave da rimuovere:

```kotlin

mappa.remove("chiave2")
```

Per accedere a un valore associato a una chiave specifica, è possibile utilizzare il metodo get() che restituisce il valore corrispondente alla chiave specificata:

```kotlin
val valore = mappa.get("chiave1")
```

Le mappe di Kotlin offrono anche funzioni utili per effettuare operazioni come la ricerca di una chiave specifica, la verifica dell'esistenza di una chiave, l'iterazione dei valori e la verifica del contenuto della mappa.

Le collezioni e le mappe di Kotlin sono estremamente utili per gestire e manipolare i dati in modo efficiente e flessibile. Grazie alle strutture dati offerte dalla libreria standard di Kotlin, è possibile creare e utilizzare facilmente liste, insiemi e mappe per soddisfare le diverse esigenze di programmazione.

Inoltre, Kotlin offre anche funzionalità avanzate per lavorare con collezioni e mappe, come le espressioni lambda e le funzioni di
```

estensione che consentono di scrivere codice più conciso e leggibile.

Ad esempio, è possibile utilizzare le espressioni lambda per eseguire operazioni su ogni elemento di una collezione in modo efficiente:

```kotlin
val listaNumeri = listOf(1, 2, 3, 4, 5)
listaNumeri.forEach { numero ->
println(numero) }
```

Le funzioni di estensione, invece, consentono di aggiungere metodi personalizzati alle collezioni esistenti senza dover estendere direttamente la classe:

```kotlin
fun List<Int>.somma(): Int {
    var somma = 0
    this.forEach { numero -> somma +=
numero }
    return somma
}

val listaNumeri = listOf(1, 2, 3, 4, 5)
val somma = listaNumeri.somma()
println(somma)
```

```

Le collezioni e le mappe di Kotlin sono
strumenti essenziali per la programmazione in
Kotlin e offrono un modo efficiente e
flessibile per gestire e manipolare i dati.
Grazie alle loro funzionalità avanzate e alla
loro facilità di utilizzo, le collezioni e le
mappe di Kotlin consentono ai programmatori
di scrivere codice più efficiente e
manutenibile, migliorando la qualità e la
produttività dello sviluppo software.
```

21.Unit Testing with JUnit in Kotlin

Unit testing is an essential part of software development, as it allows developers to verify that individual units of code are working correctly. In this article, we will discuss how to write unit tests using JUnit, a popular testing framework, in Kotlin, a modern and expressive programming language that runs on the Java Virtual Machine.

Setting up JUnit in a Kotlin project is straightforward. You can add the JUnit dependency to your project by including the following line in your build.gradle file:

```
testImplementation 'junit:junit:4.12'
```

Once you have included the JUnit dependency in your project, you can start writing unit tests in Kotlin. Unit tests are typically placed in a separate directory within your project, such as src/test/kotlin. You can create a new Kotlin file for your unit tests and annotate your test classes and methods with JUnit annotations.

For example, consider the following simple

Kotlin class that we want to test:

```kotlin
class MathUtils {
    fun add(a: Int, b: Int): Int {
        return a + b
    }

    fun subtract(a: Int, b: Int): Int {
        return a - b
    }
}
```

We can write unit tests for this class using JUnit. Here's an example of a JUnit test class in Kotlin:

```kotlin
import org.junit.Test
import org.junit.Assert.*

class MathUtilsTest {

    private val mathUtils = MathUtils()

    @Test
    fun testAdd() {
        assertEquals(4, mathUtils.add(2, 2))
        assertEquals(0, mathUtils.add(-2, 2))
```

```kotlin
    }

    @Test
    fun testSubtract() {
        assertEquals(0, mathUtils.subtract(2, 2))
        assertEquals(-4, mathUtils.subtract(-2, 2))
    }
}
```

In the above code snippet, we have created a test class `MathUtilsTest` that contains two test methods: `testAdd` and `testSubtract`. We annotate these methods with `@Test` to indicate that they are test methods. Within each test method, we use JUnit's `assertEquals` method to verify the expected output of the methods being tested.

Running these JUnit tests in Kotlin is simple. You can run your tests from your IDE, such as IntelliJ IDEA or Android Studio, by right-clicking on your test class and selecting "Run MathUtilsTest." Alternatively, you can run your tests from the command line using Gradle or another build tool.

Unit testing is an iterative process, and you may need to modify your tests as you make changes to your code. It's essential to run your tests frequently to catch any regressions or bugs in your code. By writing unit tests with JUnit in Kotlin, you can ensure the quality and reliability of your code base.

Unit testing is a critical practice in software development, and using JUnit in combination with Kotlin can help you write effective and reliable unit tests for your code. By writing unit tests, you can verify that individual units of code are working correctly and catch any bugs or regressions early in the development process. Happy testing!

22.Creating Android applications with Kotlin

Creating Android applications with Kotlin is an exciting and rewarding experience for developers. Kotlin is a modern programming language that is fully supported by Google for Android development. It offers a wide range of features that make coding more efficient and enjoyable.

In this guide, we will walk through the process of creating Android applications using Kotlin. We will cover everything from setting up your development environment to building a fully functional app with examples along the way.

Setting up your development environment is the first step in creating Android applications with Kotlin. To get started, you will need to download and install Android Studio, which is the official IDE for Android development. Android Studio comes with everything you need to start building Android apps, including the Kotlin plugin.

Once you have Android Studio installed, you can create a new project and choose Kotlin as the programming language. Android Studio will generate a basic project structure for you, including the necessary files and folders to get started.

Next, let's take a look at an example of a simple Android application written in Kotlin. We will create a basic app that displays a text message when a button is clicked.

```kotlin
import androidx.appcompat.app.AppCompatActivity
import android.os.Bundle
import android.widget.Button
import android.widget.Toast

class MainActivity : AppCompatActivity() {
    override fun onCreate(savedInstanceState: Bundle?) {
        super.onCreate(savedInstanceState)
        setContentView(R.layout.activity_main)

        val button = findViewById<Button>(R.id.button)

        button.setOnClickListener {
            Toast.makeText(this, "Button clicked", Toast.LENGTH_SHORT).show()
        }
```

```
        }
    }
}
```

In this example, we have a main activity class that extends AppCompatActivity. Inside the onCreate method, we set the layout for the activity and find the button by its ID. We then set a click listener on the button that displays a toast message when clicked.

Layout files in Android are written in XML and define the UI components for your app. Here is an example of a layout file for the activity_main.xml:

```xml
<RelativeLayout
xmlns:android="http://schemas.android.com/apk/res/android"

xmlns:tools="http://schemas.android.com/tools"
    android:layout_width="match_parent"
    android:layout_height="match_parent"
    tools:context=".MainActivity">

    <Button
        android:id="@+id/button"
        android:layout_width="wrap_content"
```

```
    android:layout_height="wrap_content"
    android:text="Click Me"
    android:layout_centerInParent="true"/>

</RelativeLayout>
```

In this layout file, we have a RelativeLayout with a single button in the center. The button has an ID that matches the one used in the Kotlin code.

Running the application in the Android emulator or on a physical device will display a button that says "Click Me". When the button is clicked, a toast message will appear with the text "Button clicked".

This is a simple example of creating an Android app with Kotlin, but there are endless possibilities for what you can build. Kotlin's concise syntax and powerful features make it a great choice for Android development.

One of the key features of Kotlin that makes it attractive for Android development is its interoperability with Java. This means that you can easily use Java libraries and frameworks in your Kotlin code, making it easier to transition from Java to Kotlin.

Another advantage of Kotlin is its null safety feature, which helps prevent null pointer exceptions at compile time. Kotlin's type system allows you to specify whether a variable can be null or not, reducing the risk of runtime crashes.

In addition, Kotlin offers many modern language features that make coding more efficient, such as data classes, coroutines for asynchronous programming, and extension functions for adding functionality to existing classes.

Here is an example of a data class in Kotlin:

```kotlin
data class User(val id: Int, val name: String)
```

Data classes in Kotlin automatically generate the standard methods like equals, hashCode, and toString, as well as component functions for destructuring.

Coroutines are a powerful feature in Kotlin for asynchronous programming. They allow you to write non-blocking code in a sequential manner, making it easier to handle tasks like network requests or database operations without blocking the main thread.

```kotlin
import kotlinx.coroutines.GlobalScope
import kotlinx.coroutines.delay
import kotlinx.coroutines.launch

fun main() {
    GlobalScope.launch {
        delay(1000)
        println("Hello, coroutines!")
    }

    Thread.sleep(2000) // wait for 2 seconds
}
```

In this example, we use coroutines to launch a new coroutine that prints "Hello, coroutines!" after a delay of 1 second. The main thread then sleeps for 2 seconds to allow the coroutine to run.

Extension functions in Kotlin allow you to add new functionalities to existing classes without modifying their source code. This is useful for adding utility methods or custom behavior to classes from third-party libraries.

Here is an example of an extension function in

Kotlin:

```kotlin
fun String.isPalindrome(): Boolean {
    return this == this.reversed()
}

fun main() {
    println("radar".isPalindrome()) // true
    println("hello".isPalindrome()) // false
}
```

In this example, we define an extension function isPalindrome for the String class that checks if the string is a palindrome. We can then call this function on any string object.

In conclusion, Kotlin is a versatile and modern programming language that is well-suited for Android development. Its concise syntax, null safety features, and interoperability with Java make it a great choice for building Android applications.

By leveraging Kotlin's features, you can create powerful and efficient Android apps with ease. Whether you are a beginner or an experienced developer, Kotlin provides a robust platform for developing innovative and high-quality Android applications.

I hope this guide has given you a good understanding of how to create Android applications with Kotlin and has inspired you to start building your own apps.

Index

Learn Kotlin

Practical Guide

A. De Quattro